Now and Then

Also by Robin Sinclair and published by Ginninderra Press
The Clouds Go Down To Heaven
Haiku Diary (Pocket Poets)

Robin Sinclair

Now and Then

Acknowledgements

'Radio Cricket' was published in *The Independent Weekly*.
'In The Silence' and 'The Heart of All' appeared in *Walking Cheerfully*, the South Australian Quaker newsletter.
'A Painting Happens' was published in *The Australian Friend*.
'The Poetry Reading' was printed in *The Poets' Republic #21*
'Blue Wren' first appeared in *Haiku Diary* in Ginninderra Press's Pockets Poets series.

Now and Then
ISBN 978 1 76041 274 6
Copyright © text Robin Sinclair 2017
Cover image is from an original oil painting by the author

First published 2017 by
GINNINDERRA PRESS
PO Box 3461 Port Adelaide 5015 Australia
www.ginninderrapress.com.au

Contents

Part One Now	7
Observations	9
Haiku	11
Spinebill	14
Walking in the Rain	15
Heatwave	16
Wonga vine, early spring	17
Flinders Ranges Haiku	18
Garden Notes	21
Birds and Animals	23
A Clutch of Collective Nouns	25
A Huddle of Little Penguins	26
An Omniscience of Godwits	27
A Stare of Owls	28
A Drift of Black Swans	29
A Skein of Geese	30
A Tidings of Magpies	31
Different	32
A Cacophony of Cockatoos	33
Blue Wren	34
A Dabble of Ducks	35
A Colony of White Ibis	36
A Fragility of Seahorses	37
A Pounce of Kittens	38
The Puppy	39
A Bewilderment of Sheep	40
A Crash of Rhinos	41
Some Observations on the Draft Horse	42
Test Driving the Kangaroo: a report	43
The Alpaca	44

Reflections	45
Elizabeth	47
Inheritance	48
The Poetry Reading	49
In the Silence	50
About Painting	51
A Painting Happens: *working notes*	52
The Heart of All	54
Part Two Then	57
Thinking about the past	59
Richard III	61
Digging Up the Roots	63
Ancestors	64
In Tasmania	65
Ancestor Stories	67
John Francis Parsons	68
Elizabeth Children and Thomas Diprose	76
The McCullochs	84
South-west Scotland	85
The McCullochs in Tasmania	88
Epitaph for James McCulloch	96
Epitaph for Rosanna McMaster McCulloch	97
Memories of Childhood	98
The Farm	99
Grandparents	103
Radio Cricket	104
Grandad's Attic	105
Storytelling	106

Part One

Now

Observations

Haiku

grey and still...
the year
getting itself into gear

young currawong
trailing its tail through a puddle...
what's this stuff?

after days of rain
a spick and span landscape
washed and rinsed and dried

anniversaries…
the year comes round again,
I think of autumn

caught up again
in sticky wisps
of technology

late summer breeze…
the apple tree shrugs off
its yellowing leaves

a lorikeet
harvesting blackberries,
silent for once

it's April…
surely enough daylight
has been saved by now?

native hens
turbocharged from whoa to go
in half a second

Spinebill

Every day the spinebill comes to the fuchsia
elegant in his chestnut vest
white shirt and black V-neck.
Wings blurring, he hovers
as his long curved beak
delicately explores each flower.

Flipping upside-down, no trouble.
When he does
the underside of his tail flickers white,
surprising us.

Probably he doesn't know about hummingbirds,
although what birds know might surprise us.
He's like one, but politer,
not so assertive,
not so much a needle zapping past the ear,
more of a graceful aerobatic acrobat.

Walking in the Rain

Hooded and raincoated I walk
head down
like a green monk.

My world of sight has shrunk
to focus on the circle at my feet
that moves along with me.
I hear the rattle of the rain against my hood,
the trickling of the ditch beside the road,
the splish of raindrops as they fall,
and underfoot the thrumming shrill of crickets.

With one good shower the creek,
so silent yesterday,
has gone from choke to chuckle.

The rain begins to slow, and stops,
and from the bushes comes the squeaky wheel
of celebrating wrens.
High in the gum trees overhead
some magpies yodel their enjoyment.

The clouds have cleared.
The half-apologetic sun of winter afternoon comes out
and in the gentle light
the tree trunks glow red-gold.

Heatwave

Too hot to go out.

In the garden grass blades crisp
and crunch like cornflakes underfoot.
Pumpkin vines and rhubarb
lie on the baking dirt
flat as a tack,
dead and lost if ever I saw it.

But at day's end
as the shadows inch across the earth
each leaf reinflates itself,
a resurrection,
only a little crispy on the edge.

Wonga vine, early spring

At eye level the frosted vine
bare and lifeless
rattles its skeleton twigs;
a few new leaves, a token outburst,
and a random spray of flowers
are telling us it's not dead yet.

But at the back
it's woven through the honeysuckle,
snaked its way right up the fence,
and twined into the neighbour's tree
a cricket pitch or more above the ground
and found a climate that it likes;
and there it celebrates,
exuberating with a flare of creamy trumpets.

The haiku

the vine reaches up
for light and warmth and life
just as we all do

Flinders Ranges Haiku

a trickle of sand
an avalanche of pebbles
      a tumble of boulders
filling the dry creek bed
with everything but water

looking for potsherds…
hunters and gatherers
of someone else's past

included among
speakers at today's meeting:
birds, she-oaks and the breeze

still as a root
the sun-seeking goanna…
but move and see him go!

in the night
the barn owl's cry
rips the fabric of the dark

small bird, big voice…
Opera in the Outback
in Brachina Gorge

the satisfaction
of identifying plants…
floramania

capturing the beauty
in a small black box
and taking it home

songs around the fire…
the musical dreamings
of many lifetimes

Garden Notes

Throughout the months of summer
we sizzled in the heat
and it dried up all the garden
till it looked quite dead and neat.
But even in the driest years
there's hope that never fails
and the first small autumn shower
brought the gardeners out like snails.

When winter came, to our delight
it settled in to rain.
It wrung our hearts to see the water
flowing down the drain;
but the tanks were overflowing,
and the reservoirs as well,
so you can't complain. *Although, of course,*
we did, as you can tell.

Well, the garden was a picture
when it came to early spring,
with the bluebells and the blossoms
and the broad beans in full swing
and the spinach and the lettuce
(*and accompanying snail*)…
We could hardly fight our way
between the parsley and the kale.

And then the weeds began to grow.
They grew with all their might,
and when we looked, the onion weed,
had doubled overnight,
and our charming woodland garden,
which we'd been so proud to own
had become a weedy jungle,
lank and rank and overgrown.

And now we've got a heatwave,
though summer's not yet here,
and things are drying out again
(The weeds may disappear!)
So here's to all us gardeners
as the next dry spell begins…
Though I've got a feeling in my bones
that nature always wins!

Birds and Animals

A Clutch of Collective Nouns

Tradition gifts to us a drift of swans,
a flick of hares, a skein of geese,
a pandemonium of parrots
and a herd of wrens.
A herd of wrens?
Can you imagine taking shelter
as a herd of wrens goes thundering past?

Peacocks, an ostentation: yes.
A bloat of hippopotami,
a crash of rhinos and a memory of elephants.

And how about
an elegance of antelopes,
a peloton of pelicans,
a flaunt of pheasants,
or a gangle of giraffes?

A Huddle of Little Penguins

A huddle of little penguins
falling over and into each other,
their white satin shirt-fronts polished by the ice,
their black velvet jackets elegant
but proof against the cold;
their little flippers
stub-like wings
flailing as they try to keep their balance on the land.

Legs? No legs.

The little leather fan-like feet
have been attached (no one knows how),
to stop them falling over.

But in the water see them go!
The word 'streamlined' invented just for them.

An Omniscience of Godwits

The god responsible for naming shore birds
was a poet,
loved words,
loved birds,
recognised a foible when he saw one.

The stilt? Well yes, it does.
Have stilts for legs.

The long-toed stint, is he curmudgeonly
and parsimonious?

And what about the dunlins, tattlers, curlews,
avocets and dotterels,
lapwings, dowitchers,
sandpipers, sanderlings, sandplovers,
yellow legs,
greenshanks, redshanks,
pratincoles and phalaropes?

And, last of all, the godwits
elegant and competent:
Perhaps they know a thing or two that we don't
looking down their supercilious bills.

A Stare of Owls

Owls are not wise in human terms.
They're simply very good at being owls.
The wide-eyed stare is focused
not on philosophy, philanthropy or cogitation
but on food.

Learn to pay attention from the owl.
Rotate your head, but otherwise be very still.
Listen
and become aware of everything
outside yourself.
Pass through the limit of your senses
to the silence that is not
and taste each sound.
Know that stillness is made up of movement,
and the dark, of flickers,
and the flickering, of life.

Then, when you are very certain,
strike.

A Drift of Black Swans

Some swans
the snowy cloud-like cousins of the north
are mute.
Black swans are not.
They flute.
They croon in soft endearments to their young.
In musical and more uplifted mode
they bugle
as they fly the moonlit night
exulting in the wide expanses of the sky.

A Skein of Geese

High in the stillness
of the evening sky
a skein of geese is going home.

A Tidings of Magpies

Sweet and clear and confident
it improvises endlessly,
fluting its compositions to the world in pure delight.

But see it stalk your garden,
arrogance in action,
watchful eye and killing beak…
is there any doubt
who's master here?

Different

The white magpie was by itself
almost invisible in the creamy grass.
It was the beak I noticed first,
a sharp and stabbing black,
and then the wary eye.

Can it know how different it is?

I waited for a while to hear it sing.
It didn't say.

A Cacophony of Cockatoos

Cockatoos are raucous and sardonic,
uncensorable, noisy and ironic,
deficient in diplomacy and tact
and modest self-effacement, that's a fact.
There's no attempt to be discreet for these,
creaking to each other in the trees.

Of all our birds, the quintessential Okker;
would rather go to cricket than to soccer;
good at sledging; ready to deride
the hopeless drongos on the other side.
At big bash, twenty-twenties, or the tests,
they flair and furl their sulphur-yellow crests
and squawk with raucous jingoistic joy,
'C'mon, you Aussie bastards! *Oy, oy, oy*!

Blue Wren

The blue wren…
just a ping-pong ball
with fashion sense

A Dabble of Ducks

It's always a surprise
that ducks can be so tall.
They sound round.

Leaving the pond
they stretch themselves
and waddle forth.

They have an air
of knowing who they are
and what they're for.

'Dabblers? Us?' they say,
'We're serious.'
But when they quack, we smile.

A Colony of White Ibis

They catch the eye, a distant flock of ibis:
puffs of cotton wool
white flowers blooming in a swamp,
a flock of clouds scudding a stormy sky.

Look closer.
Note that they're defined by black:
the sleek masked head, intent;
the tufted rump,
the stalking legs, up to the knobbly knees in mud;
the long curved pick that scavenges its world for food,
that probes each tussock,
overturns each cowpat in a search for worms,
fossicks in parks and bins for sandwich crusts
and doesn't miss a trick.

A warning:
Nature, be aware.
The auditors are here.

A Fragility of Seahorses

Tiny, dragon-like and delicate,
the head held elegantly upright
in an equine arch,
they drift
until the spiky spiral of the fine prehensile tail
wraps round a stem.

Their courtship dance
a stately and extended minuet.

The eggs, before they hatch,
are carried by the male.
Each day the female comes,
attentively,
to greet and check.
The young ones grow,
until, as perfect miniatures
they drift into the sea
to take their chance.

Of a hundred, one survives.

A Pounce of Kittens

Be glad the kitten is so small.
She'd have you pinned against the wall
before you had a chance to flee
if you were she and she were thee.

For she can pounce and she can leap
and skulk and lurk and slink and creep,
and shoot her tiny needle claws
from softly-patting pink pad paws
and in a flash, despite your screams,
Velcro her way right up your jeans.

The Puppy

He was a wolf
five hundred generations in the past
when first we met
and all of us were hunters.

Soon after that his ancestors tamed ours.

Now, when we look into this puppy's eyes
ten thousand years of life together
makes its presence felt.

A Bewilderment of Sheep

The primitive ancestral sheep
was quite astute, and liked to leap
from rocky crag to craggy knoll
on waterfall and mountain col.
Adventurous and acrobatic,
its life was joyful, though erratic.

Here you see the modern sheep.
It isn't often seen to leap
and if it wanted to, it couldn't,
and if it could, I think it wouldn't.
It likes to graze, it likes to amble.
It's fastest pace is more a scramble.

Humankind prefers sheep tame,
bland and docile, all the same.
Is it us who've lost our way?
Have we, like sheep, all gone astray?

A Crash of Rhinos

The rhino's not a laughing matter.
Snigger, and you'll end up flatter.

Trifle with a rhino
And you could end up as lino.

A simple grin
Can do you in.

The charming smile
Is sure to rile.

Don't even smirk.
It will not work.

So stay alert,
Maintain your space,

And wipe that smile
Right off your face.

Some Observations on the Draft Horse

1 The draft horse
   is connected to the earth.
   Each hoof
   thunks into place as it sets down
   like magnet meeting iron.

2 You wouldn't need a heater if you had one in the house.

3 At the front end, looking up,
   you find the liquorice and long-lashed eye
   is looking down.

4 At the back
   the coarse-haired tail flicks idly
   as the grass of yesterday
   becomes the compost of tomorrow.

Test Driving the Kangaroo: a report

A good design, though somewhat unconventional.
Well-suited to Australian outback conditions.
Can scrub-bash with efficiency,
rough bush tracks not a problem.
Has an inbuilt direction finder,
though you may occasionally find yourself
in some unexpected places.

The leaps and bounds – probably
as close to flying as you'll get
while still on earth.

Comes in a range of subtle shades.

The pocket is an excellent idea
though somewhat underutilised,
often being used for one thing only.
Other possibilities should be explored.

Takes curves well.

Acceleration from a standing start is very good.
The fuel efficiency is excellent.

The Alpaca

A body somewhat like a deer,
a graceful neck, a pricked-up ear;
a melting eye, whose glance is keener
than you'd expect; a mild demeanour…
In fact, unlike the larger llama
the mild alpaca's quite a charmer.

Reflections

Elizabeth

At ninety-one sleep comes too easily
        or not at all.
Daytime in her chair
come lambswool moments of oblivion
a drifting in and out of consciousness
dream to reality...
but which is which?

Then, late at night
        as sleep declines to call
she walks the friendly dark.
The roadside grasses stir and breathe.
Her soft old tread shuffles the moonlit dust
her stick taps out the time
and as she walks she chants
low to herself
the poems of her youth.

Inheritance

The twinkling eyes, perceptive and amused
have come down from his great-great-grandfather.
The family nose and chin,
well-known in art for starring in the portraits of the past
have likewise left their mark,
making their entry from the other side.
As for the sense of humour,
who's responsible for that?
Or the resilience,
or love of words and fear of heights?
How many generations has this smile survived intact
and can you trace its DNA?

The Poetry Reading

The used-up sun of afternoon
slants through the windows of the pub,
flattening itself in toffee-coloured slabs on floor and table.
Shadows angle off into the gloom
and in the half-light murmurs drift like dusty motes
falling among the creaking chairs and shuffling feet
and papers rustle furtively in nervous hands.

Shoulders hunched the poets wait to read.
One by one they move up to the mike.
Some are poised; they've done it all before.
Some are pale with apprehension, voices strained,
while others beam in innocent delight at their own cleverness.

And so it goes.
The room fills up with words
some of which begin to fade at once
and drift their way to a poetic limbo.
Just a few
hooked on a random twig of memory
will stay behind with us.

In the Silence

Outside it's velvet black
and quiet.
No wind tonight.
A crescent moon is hanging in a corner of the sky.

Inside
our world's contained in one small room.
The old stove crackles quietly to itself
and flames appear and disappear behind its blackening panes.
It's half shut-down
and so are we,
our heart rates slowed by silence.
Bodies drowse and thinking drifts
as dreams and meditations find their way
and take us to another place.
We read, or write, or pray.
Somebody's pencils glide and skritch
in search of a mandala.
Somebody turns with reverent curiosity
the pages that will take them into Jung's unconscious mind.
Stitch by stitch and row by row
a jumper grows.
The nimble needles dart and flicker through the wool,
weaving dreams and hopes.

And then, the bell for epilogue, three times.
Into the stillness comes the sweet and plaintive music of the flute.

About Painting

From mind's eye to hand to brush
by way of the imagination;
filtered by experience,
translated by technique,
and in the end
expressed through intuition
in a brush stroke.

A Painting Happens: *working notes*

A head full of ideas.
One is drawn out, and drawn out on to paper, tentative spider lines.
Push and pull the composition…that looks right.
Take a new canvas. Sweeps of charcoal rubbed and spread with fingers,
darks expanded and erased.
Pungent whiffs of fixative to hold the web of lines in place, then pause…
A nervous hesitation. Take the brush.
A wash of ochre, blue and violet shadows, red earth red.
Excitement grows. Another brush, a handful.
Strokes of wet paint into wet and, fugitive, the shapes appear in painty wash,
Lights and darks, highs and lows and glows.
A half-seen glimpse of accidental brilliance.
A painting has begun.

Days pass. The picture grows.
Absorbing spells of concentrated stillness,
Flurries of brush strokes, deft, decisive, clumsy.
The whispered rasp of brush on canvas,
Satisfying and pervasive smells of turps and oil,
Painty fingers, cold half-cups of coffee, smudge of cobalt on the chin.
Each stroke is both experiment and lesson. Colours change.
A face leaps out, a hand dissolves.
Today's mistake becomes the underpainting for tomorrow's new idea.
At last the brush goes down. It's done.
'This is the best that I can do.'
Stand back and look, part satisfaction, part regret.
'Is this the best that I can do?'

The Heart of All

Late March
and the dry tail of summer whispers through the scratchy grass
dragging in untidy heaps
       the used-up leaves and awkward sprawls of bark
and stirring dusty wafts of eucalyptus.

Into the afternoon a stillness falls.
The leaves forget to rustle
       and the birdcalls hush.
Even the crow's sardonic comment fades away.

Out of the hush a wind begins to stir,
       a tremor at the edge of hearing,
and in the trees
       as breezy fingers shiver up the trunks
the gum leaves rattle
       and the storm begins:
the sudden-darkening sky,
the heavy drops of rain that flail the dirt
       and quench the dust they stir.
New-rinsed
       the leaves reveal a hundred subtle shades
and underfoot the crickets shrill to life.

The heart of it, the stillness.

*

In the Meeting stillness holds.
Alone we seek the space within,
      together find it.
Moth-like our memories and thoughts obscure the light we seek.
They settle, and the space that's left begins to fill
      with living stillness.
Words we hear or speak float briefly
and fall back into the silence.

The heart of it, the stillness
at the beginning and the end of all,
the velvet hush that holds within itself the seed of life,
the tiny space that holds the universe,
the quiet that contains all speech,
      all song,
all wild exuberance of sound,
the nothing yet made up of everything.

The heart of all, the stillness.

Part Two

Then

Thinking about the past

Richard III

Six hundred years he stalked the halls
of legend, so we all recall;
Richard III, the Hunchback King,
remembered chiefly for one thing:
the murder of his nephews in the Tower,
a step he needed for his rise to power.

But is this story true, or is it spin:
a Tudor smear campaign to take us in?

Shakespeare, who loved a lively plot,
took it and ran; and so the world forgot
> *that things are seldom black and white,*
> *(and who can tell which side is right?)*
> *No one is evil through and through;*
> *and a good story isn't always true.*

So, Richard: was he much maligned,
his reputation undermined
to make the Tudor kings look good?
Was he, perhaps, misunderstood?

Over the years supporters tried
to clear his name, restore the pride.
Bit by conscientious bit
they piled up evidence that fit
a loyal king for troubled times,
not one who'd do such fearful crimes.

And then, last year they found his bones:
a council car park. (Who'd have known?)
They dug him up and checked him out
in order to remove all doubt;
studied the bones, looked at the DNA,
rebuilt the skull…his portrait, we can say,
matches it well. And then, the final call:
and, Yes! It's Richard, crooked spine and all.

The question, in the end, remains the same:
Was he the good or evil player in the game?
We have his skull, or so the experts said…
But who knows what went on inside his head?

History
remains a mystery;
the half-remembered, half-invented tales that skew our views
and twist the tails of those who read them.
Who can we believe? Who can we trust
when those who lived it all are gone to dust?

Digging Up the Roots

There's a glamour about the past
and a mystery;
a puzzle that needs to be solved,
that draws us in,
that keeps us looking,
that leads us to the Net that has no bottom
and the suitcase in the ceiling space that does;
the yellowing letters with no dates
and signed by *name illegible*;
the fading photos, carefully preserved,
with no accompanying notes
because they all knew who they were.

And when we pin them down,
those names,
those dates,
and hang them on the family tree
we feel triumphant.
'My ancestors were pioneers,' we say.
Or even better, convicts.
But when we look we see
that what we've got is just a fraction of the whole,
one or two strands out of a dozen,
or a hundred.
And where are all the rest?

Ancestors

All of us can trace our ancestry
right back to Charlemagne,
so they say,
Edward the Third, or Ghengis Khan;
thereby acknowledging the strands of lineage that interweave
 and overlap
to make the complex pattern that encompasses us all,
making us cousins by the blood,
the hair, the eyes,
the quirks that come and go and disappear and then resurface
 generations later
bouncy as a cat.

So could it be those early Israelites
were onto something when they tied us back to Adam
and, of course, to Eve?
And did their storytellers, bards and fable-makers,
busy turning myth to history and history to myth,
recognise the common thread
that ties us all together?

In Tasmania

Ancestor Stories

My parents told us stories of our Tasmanian pioneer ancestors. To us, as children living in the now, they seemed as far away as the mountains and as remote as stars.

The older I get the closer they come, till now it seems half probable that I might meet them somewhere on a back road coming round the corner in a creaking bullock dray.

Here, for my children and grandchildren, are some of their stories as I imagine them to be: a framework of all the facts and dates I know with the incorporation of some family legends and an imaginative reconstruction of how it might have been.

*

John Francis Parsons was not the first of the ancestors to arrive, but his was the story that I started with, the one that first caught my imagination. He was just twelve years old when he made his solitary and desperate bid to find a better life.

John came from somewhere in the west of England. Details are scanty and John seemed to prefer to keep it that way.

John Francis Parsons

1823–1903

Twelve years old; done with education,
maybe never had a lot,
and after his Welsh mother died
left to the mercies of a stepmother he loathed.
Desperate, he ran away to sea (easy if you lived near Bristol).
Did he know where he was going?
Did he even care
as long as it was somewhere else?

Became a ship's boy, offsider to the carpenter:
a good career move
though he didn't know it at the time.

A sailing ship, crowded and creaking;
halfway round the world on a six-month journey
that seemed to last forever;
probably storms, probably seasick, probably even homesick,
not much food, no space to move, no privacy,
uncertain and afraid.

As soon as they reached Hobart Town he left the ship
and ran.

Van Diemen's Land:
the beautiful island at the end of the world
named for a Dutchman by a Dutchman who was passing by;
noticed by Captain Cook;
touched on, quite gently, by the French;
then claimed and settled by the British in the early
Eighteen-hundreds;
a clumsy beginning with a shipload or two of convicts,
plenty of military back-up
and a handful of free settlers.

All of them knew about the local people.
Naturalists noted their habits, marvelled, drew and classified,
much as they did with wallabies and wild flowers.
If they could have pressed them in a book
or sent them, dried or pickled, back to Europe,
they would have.
Sometimes they did.
But on the whole the land's inhabitants,
(here for twenty thousand years at least),
were an embarrassment.
A settler taking up his land, laying claim and building fences,
found them in the way.

But by the time young John arrived,
1835,
they weren't a problem any more,
being either dead or banished.

So here's his ship, sailing up the Derwent
and into harbour,
mercifully free at last of gales and tossing seas.
Behind the now-established town the mountain looms,
the native bush that clothes it drawing back its skirts
to make way for the settlement.

His plan, to get as far away as possible from everything
and everyone who knows him;
So, out of the bustling raucous port
with passengers and cargo spilling off the ships that come and go
between the old world and the new,
he runs;
easy to disappear, easy to lose himself.

He finds a road that's heading out
and goes,
travelling with farmers in their loaded carts,
and settlers with their worldly goods packed tight, roped down
or dangling at the side of creaking, groaning wagons;
Passing them are horsemen,
hunters out with packs of dogs for kangaroo and wallaby;
gangs of convicts and their overseers,
soldiers, loud and bored
and just as wary of this land as anybody else.

Away from town the crowds thin out.
John can blend; he knows a thing or two, learnt on the ship.
He lends a hand, hitches a ride, works for a meal.
A boy can fit in where an adult can't.
A boy can go invisible

Bit by bit he travels north,
planning to go as far as roads will take him
and the roads aren't bad
with convict labourers to push them out and keep them up.
Up through the Midlands;
Every now and then a solitary house,
a farm, some sheep,
a little town,
some cottages, an inn, a courthouse, all in stone.
Like home but not like home.

Wary,
he keeps an eye out for the soldiery,
the right hand of officialdom.

Eventually he reaches Launceston,
another fledgling settlement
but bustling now, and prosperous for some.
Streets and houses spring up by the day
scrambling up the hillside from the wharf
and hopeful settlers come by every boat:
tinkers, tailors, labourers and farmers,
tradesmen, blacksmiths, carpenters,
every one an eager opportunist
looking for a start in this new land.

A good place to get lost, he thinks,
or find himself…

But somehow word has come ahead.
He's on a list, 'Deserters',
of some official with the will to do him in.
His punishment: a treadmill.
At least he isn't sent back to the ship
but this is just as bad.
Despair…
Trudging endlessly he has the time to make a vow:
He'll not be caught again.

So when he's done he runs again,
this time to the west
where roads and settlements are striking out into the bush.
He thinks it might be politic to change his name…or maybe
someone hears it wrong and writes it down as Pearson.
Anyway, it helps.

Bit by bit he works his way from settlement to farm,
from Hadspen, west; to Deloraine, and then the push inland
towards the mountains of the Western Tiers.
There's always work, for everybody needs some kind of home
and he has skills he learnt on board the ship.
Never any lack of wood, for trees are free
and beams and rafters, palings, shingles for the roof
are all to hand if you know how.

He makes enough to buy a modest plot of land
and build a house himself.
He's twenty and it's time to settle down.
In 1844 he marries Susan Ryder.

Susan came from Devon with her mum and sisters,
following their father Joseph
who got a one-way ticket to Van Diemen's Land:
transported there for life.
Joseph was a ploughman back in Haberton,
not far from Totness and the mists and bogs of Dartmoor.
What the government did not provide, the good Lord did.
He stole a sheep to feed his growing family
because, if you are desperate
a sheep can look much like a welfare cheque.

So Joseph came to VDL for life
and ten years later got his own life back.
His wife and daughters came,
and he took up where he'd left off
a ploughman once again,
but at the bottom of the world.

So Susan married John.

The little farming settlements had spread,
back through the watery plains,
the rolling hills pocked here and there with caves,
and up into the foothills of the Western Tiers.
Caveside: that's where John and Susan made their home;
winter rains, and frosts, and mists that drifted down the
    mountain side…

Ten years later, settled now with wife and farm and daughters,
rumours came that on the Mainland gold was found.

News of gold moves fast; a kind of epidemic.
Settlers, already on the move and open to the new
succumb quite readily
and so did John.

Crossing the Strait with others flooding in
he got to Ballarat and made a claim.
Luckier than most, he did find gold,
and loyaler than some, he took it home.
At least one trip he made enough
to heap a plate with sovereigns, a pyramid of gold,
and there were more trips and more gold.

He bought more land
until they had two hundred acres
stretching out along the foothills of the Tiers.
They called it 'Tiger Hill'
because the bush he now called his
had thylacines as well as wallabies and roos
and devils, possums, bandicoots and quolls
(which liked the vegie garden and the chooks as much as he
    and Susan did.
They thought they had a right to what he grew
since it was on their patch.)
Trapping them became an extra source of income.
Legends say he had a waistcoat of Tasmanian Tiger skin.
The thylacine is now extinct.

Over the years their family grew to twelve;
six living sons and two more girls.
The boys were farmers, hunters, trappers, improvisers, good at making do,
men of a multitude of useful skills just like their dad.
With him they pioneered the trackways of the Tiers,
carrying supplies up to the plateau for the men who worked there.
Still on the maps today are Parsons Track and Parsons Falls.

From Ballarat John brought home more than gold.
He got a taste for rum.
Back at home he visited the inn at Chudleigh far too often.
What he'd earned and built began to drain away into the coffers of the pub.
Susan and the boys would grit their teeth,
and harness up the horse and trap to bring him home.
Good Methodists they were, or all became,
the evils of the drink quite real to them.
At last they made him sign some papers
that gave over all to their control.

He died at eighty,
having never tried to re-establish contact with his relatives at home,
or answer their requests for news.
His life was here.

Elizabeth Children and Thomas Diprose

In the year that John Parsons was born another family was making the decision that would turn their lives and their world upside down, taking them from Kent in the south-east of England to the twenty-year-old colony in Van Diemen's Land.

Elizabeth Children came from a family that was Kentish to the bones and her husband, Thomas Diprose, from stock that had arrived from France as refugees several hundred years before. No doubt he felt as Kentish as she did; but much as they may have loved it, the times and the place were not good for them and their growing family.

By early 1800
the Children family had been in Headcorn, Kent
at least six hundred years.
The Saxons named their settlement *caeld-ern*, 'the cold place',
and over centuries it turned to Children's Farm.
The family were Kentish yeomen, solid and respectable.
They knew their worth.

Elizabeth, strong-minded, independent,
threw it all away.
She 'ran off with the coachman', so the story says.
Another thing: he was a Baptist,
not C. of E., as people ought to be.
The family was not well-pleased.
They cut her off.

In spite of that (or maybe for that reason),
she married him,
Thomas Diprose, coachman, farmer,
descendant of the Huguenots
who fled from France three hundred years before.
De Preaux they were, but in the course of time,
and in the English way
it settled out to Diprose.

They farmed.
They had eight children.
Times were difficult and crops were sparse,
and in that post-Napoleonic War time many people did it hard.
In 1823 they pulled up roots,
packed up their goods
and, gambling on a better life in a new land,
set sail for VDL.
The Childrens, who had long forgiven her,
lost patience once again.
How could she take her family to a convict colony,
and one so far away, so dangerous?

Thomas and Elizabeth had planned their venture with
    another family,
their Shoobridge cousins,
so that they had at least each other for support
and company.

The Shoobridges left first.
The voyage out was long and hard;
six months of gales and storms and illness,
the captain a martinet, with food and water rationed beyond reason.
On the way the family had to watch three of the children and their mother
die from illness and privation.

Word of this had not reached Kent before the Diprose family left
and so they carried on as planned.
A family of ten, they travelled steerage from necessity,
hardly space to turn around.
The ship was overcrowded, deck space shared with sheep and cattle.
For Thomas and Elizabeth arriving with the family whole
was an achievement in itself.

The colony was barely twenty.
Hobart Town had marked its territory with squared-off streets
and sandstone buildings, solid in the Georgian style
and meant to last.
The convicts and the military had done their work
in setting up the place,
and now free settlers flooded in,
taking up the park-like hinterland for flocks and crops.

To make a claim you had to prove your worth;
A list of goods and money was required.

What they brought:
> *A plough, and what goes with it*
> *Ironmongery*
> *Scythes and sickles, sacks and sundry*
> *Horse gear: harness, saddles, bridles*
> *Utensils for the dairy*
> *Copper, churn*
> *Earthenware and china, glass and plate*
> *Seed corn and hop sets*
> *Books*
> *Money, Forty pounds*
> *Firearms*
> *Bedsteads and mattresses*
> *Linen and weaving*
> *Total worth four hundred and eighty-four pounds*

Not a lot; but in the end they got a grant:
500 acres, which they had to choose
from what was then available.

Most of the choicest sites, close to Hobart Town or rivers,
had been claimed early by more wealthy colonists.
The land that Thomas chose was at the limit of the Midlands
on the edge of Epping Forest,
near to the road, or track, that went from Hobart Town to
 Launceston.
The land was a flattish, a tree-dotted plain.
The Western Tiers loomed on the skyline.
Water for stock and irrigation came from a lagoon
that tended to dry out in summer.
The family had a well close to the house.
They liked their land.
Elizabeth described it in a letter home,
'*Park-like…fertile…wonderful.*'
They called it Iberden in memory of Kent.

They built a house, planted a garden,
ploughed and fenced and settled in.
Peach trees and almonds that they planted flourished.

Another list of what they had:

> Elizabeth: *a sharp tongue but a heart of gold.*

Well, you could tell that from the first as she defied her family,
knowing what she wanted: Thomas.
And the way she stayed with him,
supporting to the end.

> *Thomas: a great capacity for work*
> *and the ability to see beyond his own backyard.*

> *Courage*, both of them,

to take the family to a place almost unknown, and dangerous.

      Their *faith*, considerable,
in the Lord, their church, each other.
There were dangers.
Bushrangers: convicts who'd escaped and lived
by living off the lives and goods of others,
nothing to lose and desperate;
often pillaging the farms they knew and maybe where they'd worked,
slave labourers.
Escaped, they took their wages out in plunder.
At the Diprose house they found Elizabeth at home.
Unfazed, she gave them bread and then the sharp end of her tongue,
after which she read the Bible to them,
after which they left.

Then there were Blacks, the Aborigines whose land it was
or had been,
fenced out of their hunting grounds,
pursued and persecuted,
driven out by some, though treated well by others…
but what are clothes and flour to those who've lost their land,
    their rights, their culture?
They did as desperation drove them to,
attacking, killing, sometimes burning.
Soon they were gone entirely,
the last sad remnants driven off and sent away.

No Blacks, no problem.
Pretty soon, no convicts either.
The colony was left to settle out, evolving and transforming as it grew.
From the mixed bag of hopes and fears and aspirations,
courage and cowardice,
daring, desperation,
prejudice and vision;
from the best and worst of human life the colony would grow.

Twenty years Elizabeth and Thomas lived and worked at Iberden
before they left to spend their final years in Launceston.
Their family grew up, married,
left to make their own lives in this land that now was theirs;
to swell the population, which they did,
more than successfully.

Elizabeth and Thomas were in their eighties when they died.
In coming here
they left behind their families, their heritage,
their place in life,
and found another, and a place in history.

Footnote

'It was the women in our family who were strong',
my Nanna said.
What did she mean by strength?
Where does it come from: bred into the bone,
or brought to life by circumstance
until it leaps out fully formed to meet a challenge?
If Elizabeth is anything to go by
stubbornness comes into it,
facing her family down to marry Thomas
and later on, with absolute assurance,
putting in their place the bushrangers who came to call.
Underneath her serviceable skirt
did her knees ever knock?
Or did she have a moment of self-doubt?
In true colonial style
a backbone made of steel and whalebone held her up.

The McCullochs

The family I heard most about were the McCullochs, my father's family. He loved to tell their stories. By the time they arrived in 1855, thirty-two years after the Diproses and twenty after John Parsons, Van Diemen's Land had become Tasmania, a well established colony, and no more convicts were arriving.

In re-creating this story I have reached back to try to imagine what Galloway, the corner of south-west Scotland which they left to come here, might have been like and how it became that way. Several thousand years have been telescoped into seventy lines. I apologise to the people and facts that fell by the wayside.

The back story: where they came from and what it might have been like.

South-west Scotland

5000 BC to AD 1800

Twenty miles they came, those far-off ancestors,
crossing the strip of sea between the world they knew in Ireland
to a new and unknown land.
Not far,
but it took them to the other side of their world,
cresting the waves in a coracle,
ghosting over the horizon,
sliding down the other side to wash up
on a granite-pebbled beach,
to see an untouched forest, old as time,
as packed with game as fleas are on a dog
and no one there but them.
They made it theirs, those Stone Age Gaels,
for a millennium or two,
and gifted it their name in Galloway.

And then the others came:
some Celts, up from the south, bringing bronze tools and
    farming,
changing their way of life.
Later some Roman troops arrived to civilise and tame
and open up their eyes to other worlds;
which led to Christianity and early saints,
who taught them holiness and how to read,
the benefits of education and a peaceful life.

Things fell apart when Vikings struck,
to raid, to conquer and to hold,
adding some other strands of DNA,
a fierce aggression and an attitude:
'What's mine is mine!
What's yours is mine as well!'

And finally, the Normans, to divide and rule
and turn them into serfs. Or try.

Out of this McCullochs came,
a fierce and stubborn mix of Viking, Gael and Celt.
They raided with the best, and worst,
and on the nearby Isle of Man the farmers had a grace that said,
'Keep me, my good corn and my sheep and my bullocks
From Satan, from sin, and those thievish McCullochs!'

After a time religious zealotry arose
replacing tribal warfare.
After all, you have to have a side to barrack for.
The Covenanters came and, with the Catholics and established
    Church
they split communities.
They hooked into the loyalties and pride and native
    stubbornness,
the fierce rambunctiousness
and, most of all,
refusal to admit that their side might be wrong.
Blood was shed, and lost, to keep the Cause
(whichever one it was)
and people died.

History does not record
McCullochs being martyred for their faith
and one at least was on the persecuting side.
The list of those who were remembered was determined by
　　the courts:
the rogues and scoundrels, or litigious ones.
Meanwhile, at home and quietly minding their own business
the rest, good citizens no doubt
got on with life without a fuss
and no one made a record of their lives.

By 1800 peace had been restored.
The Kirk's respectability prevailed.
But so did poverty, for those who scraped a living on a little
　　piece of land
or worked for others.
So when the offer of a better future came
they took the sea again;
twelve thousand miles this time,
a journey full of hopes and fears,
cresting the waves
bumping over the equator,
sliding down the other side
to find an island, full of trees and game and promise.
Tasmania.

The McCullochs in Tasmania

1855

Van Diemen's Land is gone.
Its convict past is over; not forgotten
but living on forever in descendants' genes.
To mark the change from penal site to proud free colony
the name has changed.
Abel Tasman, 1640, named it for a Dutch official,
and now it's named for him: Tasmania.

And transportation's ended. Jubilation!
What can possibly go wrong?
Suddenly there's no free source of labour.
The gangs that built the roads and bridges
and did the work that built the colony
are gone.
Needed: free settlers, lots of them!
And so in Britain Immigration Societies spring up to fill the gap.

James McCulloch, born in Ballantrae in Southern Ayrshire, 1809;
(father a tenant farmer, grandfather a Glasgow harness weaver)
and his wife Rosanna, a McMaster, daughter of a shepherd,
took their family and left with other hopeful immigrants
looking for a place they could call theirs, a new start for the family.
It meant they'd never see their native place again.

James was 44, Rosanna 43.
Their children: John, the eldest, 20,
then Hugh and James and Grace and Jane,
Andrew and Robert and the baby, Peter,3.
The *Montmorency* sailed in 1854 from Liverpool to Launceston
carrying a load of Irish, English, Germans, Scots,
all keen to start anew.
The voyage lasted 80 days without event (or so the papers said).
A speedy trip.

Once there, they found a spot and fitted in,
learning their new land and earning cash to buy their own.
The first three years they stayed near Westbury.
The men found work for Richard Dry
(reformer, premier, landholder)
as labourers and ploughmen on his land.
The youngest children went to school.
Rosanna stayed at home and did as women always do,
making a home wherever they might be; holding it all together.
Another baby came, the last: a girl, and named for her, Rosanna.

By 1859 they had the knowledge and the wherewithal
to buy land of their own,
500 acres on the Gawler River five miles from the Leven mouth,
a settlement just opening up.

With other friends, a party of nineteen,
They loaded their belongings onto bullock drays
and headed west.
It took three days to get there.
After Deloraine the road became a track through forest,
newly opened up to reach the Mersey port
so farmers' produce could be taken off by ship.
The rivulets and streams had wooden bridges, some just logs
   but serviceable,
(built by another ancestor, but that's another story).

By day two they had reached East Devon,
named by a pioneer with memories of home.
They crossed the Mersey at a narrow point
bypassing its wide mouth and growing port.
Another mile or two until they crossed the Don
and then by dray track on towards the Forth.

Waiting for low tide they ford the river at the bar.
The drays and all their goods stay dry.
Upstream a mile or so they glimpse the settlement of
   Hamilton-on-Forth,
a dozen houses on the river flats
backed by a scattering of whitened ring-barked trees.

They press on to the west along the beach,
tea-tree scrub and boobialla.
As dusk approaches, silhouetted by the setting sun
they see a range that runs down to the sea,
the Dial Range. The jutting outcrop called The Gnomon
is the pointer on the sundial.
This is a view that will be theirs for many years.

At the Leven mouth there's not a lot.
The river's wide and deep enough to take a ship
and there's a house or two and traces of a paling splitters' camp,
plus an old track that heads off south towards the Gawler River,
which is where they want to go.

They know that this track, with some work,
will take them for two miles towards their goal.
The rest is untouched bush with ti-tree thickets,
stands of acacia, silver wattle, blackwood,
ancient fallen trunks,
and looming over all, enormous stringy-barks.

The next few days are spent in hacking out a track
to take them to their block.
The work is hard.
It gives a feel for what they'll have to do for many years,
to clear their land.

After some days of work
they start the last part of the journey,
all on foot,
walking or running by the teams and urging on the bullocks.
The heavy drays bump over tussocks
creaking and groaning as they slide through mud
and inch by fallen trees.
Wallabies bound off into the scrub, birds startle and take flight.
The air fills with excited speculation.

The last camp's on their land, a flat beside the Gawler River,
really just a creek.
Behind, the land slopes up quite steeply to a plateau
which is where their fields will be;
good farming land they hope.
First job: to build themselves a house,
something that will see them through the winter.
Saplings and bark are what's to hand, and palings split from
    larger trees.
They build two largeish rooms for eating and for sleeping;
a lean-to at the end for cooking.
The rest will come with opportunity and need.

After that the clearing work begins.
Some trees are felled, some ringbarked and left standing till
 they die.
Logs are piled in heaps and burnt, or split for palings.
Once the ashes cool they sow potatoes,
their first crop.
As for meat, there's always wallaby.

The first few years they concentrate on clearing
until they've done enough to subdivide it for their sons.
It's just their group, McCullochs and nine others,
a self-contained community surrounded by the bush
with James as leader.
James is focused, works towards his goal,
doesn't mind that in their own small world they rarely see
 another soul.
It's different for Rosanna, used to daily chats with friends and
 neighbours,
exchanging news and gossip,
learning from each other how to improvise,
what you cook and eat in this new land,
what you do when little ones get sick.
Her world is bounded by the trees, the creek, the sky. The
 family.

Once a year James and the boys go back to Westbury to join
   the harvest,
earning the cash to buy the goods they need.
The women stay,
having put their orders in for all the things they can't produce:
needles, good hard-wearing cloth and thread, tea and flour and
   sugar…

Other settlers come, more Scots.
The sons and daughters (now much more Tasmanian than Scot)
grow up and marry childhood friends and neighbours.
James and Rosanna, in their cabin made of logs
first add another room as each son marries
making a kind of long-house.
But after several years the sons each have a farm, a house, a
   growing family.

They need a road for taking goods to market
but in the early years there isn't one.
Owners of the land that's closer in
decline to have a track go through their land,
so the McCullochs and their neighbours on these isolated blocks
find themselves cut off, no access to the Leven port.
After some years of protests, pleas and action
a road is built. The Edinburgh Road (what else?)
joins the Old Plank Road at Abbotsham and links them to the
   port.

A story handed down the generations
tells of the 'Auld Man', James, who
six years after they arrived was watching as his sons cut down a tree.
It fell and struck a sapling, which rebounded and struck James
and broke his leg.
When the boys arrived they found him calmly sitting up
brushing the dirt off bits of bone protruding through the skin.
The leg was broken in three places.
There was a desperate dash to fetch a neighbour several miles away
skilful at setting bones.
The leg did mend, but James at 50 years,
could never work as well again.
He supervised. Made sure his sons knew what to do, and how.
Welcomed new neighbours in,
he and Rosanna famous for their hospitality.

At 64 Rosanna died, rheumatic fever,
leaving James to feel her loss for nearly twenty years.

By the time he died in 1892, aged 81,
district and community were well-established, prosperous.
Children and descendants flourished.
There was a Presbyterian church and burial ground
on land that he had given for the purpose.
There he was buried, and Rosanna,
and their children and descendants
right down the generations to this day.

Epitaph for James McCulloch

1809–1892

A man of vision and determination,
he sought a better future for his family
and made it happen.
Hard work and courage were his watchwords.
To his family he was the patriarch,
To his community, a leader.

Epitaph for Rosanna McMaster McCulloch

1810–1874

Although she left the land where she was born
her home went with her.
She had nine children,
six sons, three daughters,
one Tasmanian born and named for her.
Resourceful, courageous and hospitable
she was a true partner with her husband
in making a new life in a new land.

Memories of Childhood

After the McCullochs had established themselves at Gawler, in north-western Tasmania, their sons and grandsons spread out into the surrounding areas. My father's father found himself some land at Preston, ten miles south of Gawler and fifteen miles south of Ulverstone on the way to the mountains. Fifty years of hard work saw the farm transformed from bush to the idyllic landscape I remember from my childhood.

The Farm

My father's farm, north-west Tasmania

Somewhere close to 1900 my grandfather,
a newly-married man with wife and life and hopes ahead,
acquired this land.
Halfway between the mountains and the sea and partly cleared
it had a rearing stony hill covered with giant gums,
a creek, a waterfall.
Clearing the bush for crops they ring-barked trees or chopped them down
and piled the massive logs in heaps with bullock teams
then burnt them, planting crops into the ashes when they cooled.
Ten miles away at night they saw the glow of fires,
a beacon of intent. 'I claim and plant this land!'

They had three sons, young boys.
The times were hard.
Newly-planted crops soon disappeared beneath a sea of rabbits,
bracken fern and blackberries.
They left it for a while to try their luck elsewhere,
farming in Gippsland for some years.
But they came back, and with their sons, now grown, they made a go of it.
They made it work by working every moment of the day,
hard work and harder work,
clearing, ploughing, planting, harvesting and building.
As a man my dad worked on that farm twelve years for board and keep.
Then, when he married it became his own.

By 1950 it was at its best.

I remember
...a looming, rounded grassy hill
that we ran up and tumbled down like puppies;
on its crest a fringe of giant stringy-barks,
survivors of the bush that fifty years before covered the land.
Some of them had hollows where we hid and played.

...watching the stars at night
from bunks on the veranda,
and the sunset, blazing gold behind the hill.

...in the winter, frosts that burst the pipes,
and one year when it snowed a foot.

...rich chocolate soil stirred into slush by cows
as they came in for milking;
mud that sucked the gumboots off our feet.

...stones, turned up in their hundreds by the plough,
rough and brown like giant spuds,
walling the paddocks,
making a ford across the creek,
piled in giant heaps.

...in the creek a pool, sun-dappled, willow-shaded,
where platypuses came and went
and where a hopeful visitor once set a rabbit trap that caught
    a fish.

...the waterfall:
...the coolness in the cave behind the fall,
the mist of spray lifting the hair;
the mat of liverwort and moss clinging to the dripping rock;
the grove of man-ferns arching overhead;

the scent of bronzed and dying fronds beneath our feet.
...everywhere, the hills and mountains:
Looming to the south and looking grim,
seriously rugged, often snow covered,
was Black Bluff;
and to the east a monolith of blue, Mount Roland.

I remember...
...the orchard planted by my grandmother,
currants and apple trees,
a quince,
gooseberries in prickly rows,
a grove of raspberries
and ancient multi-branching cherry plums.

...the vegie garden in which rhubarb leapt,
carrots exuberated, lettuces ballooned,

all fertilised by run-off as we hosed the cow-shed out.
...the chooks, so self-important, gossipy;
the pigs in mud;
the dogs, trained to bring cows for milking:
'Fetch 'em on!' my dad would yell.

…the old farmhouse
that mushroomed from a modest start in weatherboard,
sprouting verandas, extra rooms.

…the stables,
where at night the big draft horses shuffled plate-sized feet
and dozed and chomped
exuding warmth.
Lantern in hand my father checked them every night at nine.

It's all gone now.
The Forestry has done its bit
and alien gum trees march in ragged rows
all up the hill and down again.
Where did the orchard go? The house?
The bits and pieces that accompanied the lives of all of us
who lived here for a hundred years?

Last year among the trees
I found a draft horse shoe,
reminder of my father's six-horse team.

And daffodils.

Grandparents

Both sets of grandparents lived nearby. My father's father, Ern McCulloch, was the grandson of James and Roseanna McCulloch, original settlers. He retired from a lifetime of back-breaking work on the farm and drove the shop bus, making deliveries of groceries, goodwill and gossip from the general store to all the farms around the district. As small children, we often rode with him. He was a friendly, gentle man, universally liked and his visits were social occasions as much as service stops, with many cups of tea and scones. On the way home from the last farm, in the now-empty bus, we would be allowed to ride in the big tea chest that smelt deliciously of fresh bread.

Just across the paddock lived my mother's parents, Allen and Mary Parsons. Allen was the grandson of the pioneer John Francis Parson and had grown up on the family farm at Caveside, at the foot of the Western Tiers. Mary was the great-great-granddaughter of Elizabeth and Thomas Diprose. When Allen proposed to Mary, he was working on the farm and Mary, who knew that education mattered, told him to go away and get some more. He did, and became a teacher.

Grandad had been a headmaster of small country schools, but in retirement he had revisited his boyhood in creating a flourishing fruit and vegetable garden in the steep paddock behind the house which he largely built himself. It was adjacent to my father's farm, and we saw them daily.

Radio played an important part in keeping them connected to the world, as it did for most people in those days.

Radio Cricket

In Nanna's kitchen
cooking came with cricket commentary
and recipes became Macgilvrayed,
so that the biscuits, gold and crisp and warm,
were stuffed with dates and anecdotes
and spiced with reminiscences.
Turnovers browned to the turn of overs,
sponge cakes rose with scores and fell with wickets,
cups of tea occurred when drinks were taken,
and Bradman batted on
through two whole days of bottling plums.

Housework gloomily occurred when rain stopped play.

In the off-season parliament filled in,
a feeble substitute but not unlike…
Hours of stonewalling,
sledging on the side,
from time to time the umpire's call
and now and then a brilliant spark…

But all without the lure which cricket dangles
and by which we're hooked:
that something wonderful might happen any minute now!

Grandad's Attic

From Nanna's kitchen and its spicy baking smells
a small door opened to a pantry
and from the pantry rose a wooden stair.
Four steps up and then a turn, and then four more;
a push to make the trapdoor flap fall backwards with a thud…
and then the attic.
Paper smells: a different kind of spicy,
the dusty, musty, tickly scent of knowledge
cut and filed and pasted,
encoded on to charts and stored in books
and seeping out of yellowed bones and fossils;
the ghosts of chalk and years of patient teaching,
all stored because how could you throw them out?

The reverence for learning and the hankering for knowledge
never left him.
In his attic I found part of it.
He passed it on to me.

Storytelling

What makes us human?
Telling stories.

Where do stories come from?
Out of the mists of mind and time.

How do we know ourselves?
Through the window of the story
that we tell ourselves
about ourselves.

Why do we tell stories?
Because we need to wonder,
to speculate and to explain
what makes us human.

www.ingramcontent.com/pod-product-compliance
Lightning Source LLC
Chambersburg PA
CBHW070102120526
44589CB00033B/1533